Two Awesome Free Gifts For You

I want to say "Thank You" for buying my book so I've put together a few, awesome free gifts for you.

The Essential Kitchen Series Cooking Hacks & Tips Book

&

100 Delicious New Recipes

These gifts are the perfect add-on to this book and I know you'll love them.

So visit the link below to grab them now!

www.GoodLivingPublishing.com/essential-kitchen

Table of Contents

Introduction

Acai Recipes

The Essential Kitchen Series, Book 64

38 of the Best Acai Recipes for Health and Weight Loss to Burn Fat and Live Healthy

Acai berries are the fruit of acai palm trees. They are primarily grown in Central and South America but may be relatively easy to find in the frozen section of your location grocery story. They are small, delicious berries that are packed with flavor and a variety of antioxidants, giving them nutritional value for any diet. Consuming acai berries have a number of systemic benefits including increased energy levels, enhanced metabolic functions, and a bolstered immune system.

So, keeping that in mind, a step in the right direction today can make all the difference in how you feel and how your body performs tomorrow. Learn to appreciate life a little bit more, build a sense of confidence, and adopt an attitude of well-being by preparing the amazing recipes contained in this Essential Kitchen Series Recipe Book!

Welcome the Acai Recipes Cookbook into your kitchen and break free from the mainstream, free yourself from chronic pain, and cleanse your system by pledging to eat a healthy diet. You've heard a lot lately from the media, online cooking shows and your doctor about anti-oxidants and free radicals. Incorporate this newfound knowledge into your own diet by utilizing these tasty recipes.

It's a fact of life that people snack. *Acai Recipes* is a must read cookbook for individuals desiring more energy, reduced pain, and a stronger heart. Learn what thousands have already discovered in relation to inflammation: some ingredients exacerbate inflammation, while others act as healing agents.

It's your body; start the healing process today. Learn to take charge of its maintenance, turning the corner on fatigue and pain.

Acai & Strawberries Bowl

Makes: 2 servings

Ingredients:

- 7 ounce chunks, frozen acai
- ¼ cup frozen strawberries
- ¼ cup frozen blueberries
- ¼ cup frozen raspberries
- 5 peeled and sliced small bananas
- ¼ cup frozen pineapple
- ¼ cup frozen mango
- ¼ cup almond milk

For Topping:

- ¼ cup granola
- 1 sliced banana
- ¼ cup sliced fresh strawberries
- 2 sprigs fresh mint

Procedure:

In a high speed blender, add acai, strawberries, blueberries, raspberries, banana, pineapple, mango and almond milk and pulse till smooth. Transfer the mixture into a bowl. Top with granola, banana slices, strawberry slices and fresh mint and serve immediately.

Acai & Chia Seeds Bowl

Makes: 1 serving

- 7 ounce chunks, frozen acai
- ¼ cup frozen strawberries
- ¼ cup frozen blueberries
- ¼ cup frozen blackberries
- 1 of peeled and sliced small banana
- ½ cup almond milk
- 1 teaspoon chia seeds

For Topping:

- 1 sliced banana
- ¼ cup blackberries and raspberries
- 2 tablespoons nuts
- 2 tablespoons shredded coconut

Procedure:

In a high speed blender, add acai, strawberries, blueberries, blackberries, banana, almond milk and chia seeds and pulse till smooth. Transfer the mixture into a bowl. Top with banana slices, blackberries, raspberries, shredded coconut and nuts and serve immediately.

Acai & Papaya Bowl

Makes: 1 serving

- ½ cup acai smoothie pack
- ½ cup papaya
- ½ can organic pumpkin
- 1 tablespoon Maca
- 2/3of peeled and sliced small bananas
- 1 tablespoon cinnamon
- 1 cup almond milk

For Topping:

- 1 peeled and sliced small banana
- 2 tablespoons granola
- ¼ cup peeled and chopped papaya
- 2 tablespoons cashews
- 2 tablespoons goji berries
- 2 tablespoons pomegranate seeds

Procedure:

In a high speed blender, add unsweetened acai smoothie pack, papaya, organic pumpkin, Maca, banana and almond milk and pulse till smooth. Transfer the mixture into a bowl. Top with banana slices, granola, papaya, cashews, goji berries and pomegranate seeds and serve immediately.

Acai & Pineapple Bowl

Makes: 1 serving

Ingredients:

- ½ cup acai smoothie pack
- ½ cup frozen pineapple
- ½ of peeled and sliced small bananas
- ¾ cup chopped kale
- ½ cup frozen mango
- 1 teaspoon Maca powder
- ½ cup granola
- ¼ cup coconut milk

For Topping:

- ½ peeled and sliced small banana
- ¼ cup granola
- 1 tablespoon goji berries
- 3-4 thinly sliced strawberries
- ¼ cup chopped fresh mango
- ½ cup sliced pineapple
- 2 teaspoons cacao nibs

Procedure:

In a high speed blender, add acai smoothie pack, pineapple, banana, kale, mango, Maca powder, granola and coconut milk and pulse till smooth. Transfer the mixture into a bowl. Top with banana slices, granola, goji berries, sliced strawberries, mango, pineapple and cacao nibs and serve immediately.

Acai & Peanut Butter Bowl

Makes: 1 serving

Ingredients:

- ½ cup acai smoothie pack
- 1 of peeled and sliced small banana
- ½ cups frozen berries
- 2 tablespoons peanut butter
- ½ cup granola
- ¼ cup yogurt

For Topping:

- ½ cup granola
- ½ of peeled and sliced small banana
- 2 tablespoons peanut butter
- ¼ cup cacao nibs

Procedure:

In a high speed blender, add acai smoothie pack, banana, berries, peanut butter, granola and yogurt and pulse till smooth. Transfer the mixture into a bowl. Top with granola, banana slices, peanut butter and cacao nibs and serve immediately.

Acai & Banana Bowl

Makes: 1 serving

Ingredients:

- ½ cup acai smoothie pack
- 1 of peeled and sliced small banana
- ¼ cup blueberries
- ¼ cup raspberries
- ¼ cup blackberries
- ½ cup granola
- ½ cup almond milk

For Topping:

- ½ cup granola
- 1 of peeled and sliced small banana
- 2 tablespoons chopped blueberries

Procedure:

In a high speed blender, add acai smoothie pack, banana, blueberries, raspberries, blackberries granola and almond milk and pulse till smooth. Transfer the mixture into a bowl. Top with granola, banana slices and chopped blueberries and serve immediately.

Acai & Raw Chocolate Bowl

Makes: 1 serving

Ingredients:

- ½ cup acai smoothie pack
- 1 of peeled and sliced small banana
- 1 tablespoons cacao powder
- ½ of peeled and sliced small avocado
- 1 cup frozen berries
- ½ cup spinach
- 2 tablespoons agave nectar
- ½ cup almond milk

For Topping:

- 2 tablespoons hemp seeds
- 2 tablespoons cacao nibs
- 2 tablespoons flax seeds
- 2 tablespoons bee pollen
- 1 peeled and sliced small banana

Procedure:

In a high speed blender, add acai smoothie pack, banana, cacao powder, avocado, berries, spinach, agave syrup and almond milk and pulse till smooth. Transfer the mixture into a bowl. Top with hemp seeds, cacao nibs, flax seeds, bee pollen and sliced banana and serve immediately.

Acai & Kiwi Bowl

Makes: 1 serving

- ½ cup acai smoothie pack
- 1 peeled and sliced small banana
- 1 tablespoons cacao powder
- ½ of peeled and sliced small kiwi
- ¼ cup blueberries
- ¼ cup strawberries
- 1 cup granola
- 2 tablespoons agave nectar
- ½ cup almond milk

For Topping:

- ¼ cup chopped pineapple
- ¼ cup chopped mango
- ¼ sliced cup strawberries, sliced
- ¼ cup blueberries
- ½ of peeled and sliced small kiwi
- 1 peeled and sliced small banana

Procedure:

In a high speed blender, add acai smoothie pack, banana, cacao powder, kiwi, blueberries, strawberries, granola, agave syrup and almond milk and pulse till smooth. Transfer the mixture into a bowl. Top with pineapple, mango, strawberries, blueberries, kiwi and sliced banana and serve immediately.

Acai Green Bowl

Makes: 1 serving

Ingredients:

- ½ cup acai smoothie pack
- 1 peeled and sliced small banana
- ½ cup chopped mango
- 1 cup kale
- 1 cup spinach
- ½ of peeled and sliced small avocado
- ½ cup almond milk

For Topping:

- ¼ cup granola
- 2 tablespoons shredded coconut
- 2 tablespoons sesame seeds
- 2 tablespoons hemp hearts
- 1 peeled and sliced small banana

Procedure:

In a high speed blender, add acai smoothie pack, banana, mango, kale, spinach, avocado and almond milk and pulse till smooth. Transfer the mixture into a bowl. Top with granola, coconut, sesame seeds, hemp hearts and sliced banana and serve immediately.

Acai & Coconut Bowl

Makes: 1 serving

- ½ cup pure acai juice
- 1 peeled and sliced small banana
- 2 tablespoons shredded coconut
- 1 cup strawberries
- ½ cup blueberries
- 2 tablespoons agave nectar
- ½ cup coconut milk

For Topping:

- 2 tablespoons chia seeds
- 2 tablespoons granola
- 2 tablespoons coconut chips

Procedure:

In a high speed blender, add pure acai juice, banana, coconut, strawberries, blueberries, agave nectar and coconut milk and pulse till smooth. Transfer the mixture into a bowl. Top with chia seeds, granola and coconut chips and serve immediately.

Acai Super-Food Breakfast Bowl

Makes: 1 serving

Ingredients:

- ½ cup frozen acai puree
- 1 peeled and sliced small banana
- 2 tablespoons cubed mango
- 1 cup raspberries
- ½ cup blueberries
- 2 tablespoons agave nectar
- ½ cup almond milk

For Topping:

- 1 medium peeled and cubed mango
- 1 tablespoon goji berries
- 2 tablespoons slivered almonds
- 1 teaspoon black sesame seeds
- 1 tablespoon coconut chips
- 2 tablespoons granola
- 1 teaspoon cacao nibs

Procedure:

In a high speed blender, add acai purre, banana, mango, raspberries, blueberries, agave nectar and almond milk and pulse till smooth. Transfer the mixture into a bowl. Top with mango, goji berries, almonds, black sesame seeds, coconut chips, granola and cacao nibs and serve immediately.

Acai & Pumpkin Bowl

Makes: 1 serving

Ingredients:

- ½ cup frozen acai puree
- 1 peeled and sliced small banana
- ¾ cup pumpkin puree
- ½ cup strawberries
- ½ cup blackberries
- 2 tablespoons agave nectar
- 1 tablespoons granola
- ½ cup almond milk

For Topping:

- 1 tablespoon chia seeds
- 1 tablespoon coconut chips
- 1 tablespoon goji berries
- 1 tablespoon pumpkin seeds

Procedure:

In a high speed blender, add acai puree, banana, pumpkin puree, strawberries, blackberries, agave nectar, granola and almond milk and pulse till smooth. Transfer the mixture into a bowl. Top with chia seeds, coconut chip, goji berries and pumpkin seeds and serve immediately.

Acai & Mint Ice Cream

Makes: serving

Ingredients:

- 2 tablespoons acai powder
- 1 cup mixed berries
- 5 peeled and sliced small bananas
- 2 fresh mint leaves

For Topping:

- ¼ cup sliced kiwi
- ¼ cup mixed berries
- 2 mint leaves

Procedure:

In a high speed blender, add acai powder, mixed berries, bananas, and mint leaves and pulse till thick like an ice cream. Transfer into a bowl. Top with kiwi, mixed berries and mint leaves and serve immediately.

Acai Berry & Cashews Ice Cream

Makes: 1serving

Ingredients:

Ingredients:

- 1 cup raw cashews, soaked in water overnight
- 2 tablespoons acai powder
- 2 peeled and sliced small bananas
- 1 cup blueberries
- ½ cup blackberries
- ½ cup coconut milk
- 2 fresh mint leaves

For Topping:

- 1 peeled and sliced small banana

Procedure:

In a high speed blender, add soaked cashews, cashews, acai powder, bananas, blueberries, blackberries, coconut milk and mint leaves and pulse till thick like an ice cream. Transfer into a bowl. Top with banana flowers and serve immediately.

Acai Berry & Raspberries Ice Cream

Makes: 2 servings

Ingredients:

- 2 tablespoons acai powder
- 2 sliced bananas
- 1 cup raspberries
- ¼ cup acai berries
- 1 cup almond milk

For Topping:

- ¼ cup sliced frozen raspberries

Procedure:

In a high speed blender, add acai powder, bananas, raspberries, acai berries and almond milk and pulse till thick like an ice cream. Transfer into a bowl. Top with sliced frozen raspberries and serve immediately.

Acai Berry & Banana Ice Cream

Makes: 2 servings

Ingredients:

- 3 tablespoons acai berry powder
- 1 ½ cups mixed berries
- 6 of peeled and sliced small bananas
- 1 cup almond milk

For Topping:

- ¼ cup dried blueberries
- 2 peeled and sliced small bananas

Procedure:

In a high speed blender, add acai berry powder, mixed berries, bananas and almond milk and pulse till thick like an ice cream. Transfer into a bowl. Top with dried blueberries and bananas and serve immediately.

Acai Berry & Goji Berry Ice Cream

Makes: 1serving

Ingredients:

- 2 tablespoons acai berry powder
- ½ cup raw cacao nib powder
- 2 of peeled and sliced small avocados
- 1 cup goji berry powder
- 5 of peeled and sliced small bananas
- ½ cup almond milk

For Topping:

- ¼ cup dried goji berries

Procedure:

In a high speed blender, add acai berry powder, cacao powder, avocado, goji berry powder, bananas and almond milk and pulse till thick like an ice cream. Transfer into a bowl. Top with goji berry and serve immediately.

Acai Berry & Strawberries Ice Cream

Makes: 1serving

Ingredients:

- 2 tablespoons acai berry powder
- ½ cup strawberries
- ¼ cup blueberries
- ¼ cup blackberry
- 5 of peeled and sliced small bananas
- ½ cup coconut milk

For Topping:

- ¼ cup sliced strawberries
- 4 to 5 blueberries
- 2 tablespoons flax seeds
- 2 tablespoons bee pollen

Procedure:

In a high speed blender, add acai berry powder, strawberries, blueberries, blackberries, bananas and coconut milk and pulse till thick like an ice cream. Transfer into a bowl. Top with strawberries, blueberries, flax seeds and bee polled and serve immediately.

Acai Berry & Blackberries Ice Cream

Makes: 1 serving

Ingredients:

- 2 tablespoons acai berry powder
- 1 cup blackberries
- 2peeled and sliced small bananas
- ½ cup almond milk

For Topping:

- 2 to 3 blackberries

Procedure:

In a high speed blender, add acai berry powder, blackberries, bananas and almond milk and pulse till thick like an ice cream. Transfer into a bowl. Top with blackberries and serve immediately.

Acai Berry & Watermelon Ice Cream

Makes: 1 servings

Ingredients:

- 2 tablespoons acai berry powder
- ¼ cup double cream
- 1 cup mixed berries
- ½ cup decided watermelon
- ½ cup coconut milk

For Topping:

- ¼ cup craved watermelon balls
- 2 mint leaves

Procedure:

In a high speed blender, add acai berry powder, double cream, mixed berries, watermelon and coconut milk and pulse till thick like an ice cream. Transfer into a bowl. Top with watermelon balls and mint leaves and serve immediately.

Acai Berry & Fig Ice Cream

Makes: 2 servings

Ingredients:

- 4 tablespoons acai berry powder
- 1 cup coconut cream
- 4of peeled and sliced small bananas
- 1 ½ cup fresh organic figs
- 4 teaspoons goji berries

For Topping:

- 2 tablespoons bee pollen
- 2 tablespoons shredded coconut
- 2 tablespoons raw cacao nibs

Procedure:

In a high speed blender, add Acai berry powder, coconut cream, bananas, fig and goji berries and pulse till thick like an ice cream. Transfer into a bowl. Top with bee pollen, shredded coconut and raw cacao and serve immediately.

Acai Berry & Mango Ice Cream

Makes: 2 servings

Ingredients:

- 3 tablespoons acai berry powder
- 1 cup cubed mango
- 1 cup raspberries
- 3 tablespoons peanut butter
- 1 tablespoon cacao nib powder
- 1 cup coconut milk

For Topping:

- ¼ cup frozen raspberries
- 2 tablespoons coconut chips
- 2 tablespoons quinoa puffs

Procedure:

In a high speed blender, add acai berry powder, mango, raspberries, peanut butter, cacao nib powder and coconut milk and pulse till thick like an ice cream. Transfer into 2 bowls. Top with raspberries, coconut chip, quinoa puffs and serve immediately.

Acai Berry & Pineapple Ice Cream

Makes: 1 serving

Ingredients:

- 2 tablespoons acai berry powder
- ½ cup cubed pineapple
- 1 cup raspberries
- 2 tablespoons peanut butter
- 1 peeled and sliced banana
- ½ cup coconut milk

For Topping:

- ¼ cup frozen acai berries
- 1 peeled and sliced banana

Procedure:

In a high speed blender, add acai berry powder, pineapple, raspberries, peanut butter, sliced banana and coconut milk and pulse till thick like an ice cream. Transfer into a bowl. Top with Acai berries and sliced bananas and serve immediately.

Acai Berry & Avocado Ice Cream

<u>Makes</u>: 1 serving

Ingredients:

- 2 tablespoons acai berry powder
- ½ cup cubed avocado
- 1 cup raspberries
- ½ cup blueberries
- 2 tablespoons peanut butter
- 1 tablespoon cacao nib powder
- ½ cup coconut milk

<u>For Topping:</u>

- ¼ cup cacao nibs

Procedure:

In a high speed blender, add acai berry powder, avocado, raspberries, blueberries, peanut butter, cacao nib powder and coconut milk and pulse till thick like an ice cream. Transfer into a bowl. Top with cacao nibs and serve immediately

Acai Green Smoothie

Makes: 1 serving

Ingredients:

- ½ cup frozen acai berry puree
- 1 cup baby spinach
- 1 tablespoon raw cacao nib powder
- ¼ cup strawberries
- 1of peeled and sliced small banana
- ½ cup almond milk

For Topping:

- 1 tablespoon raw cacao nib

Procedure:

In a high speed blender, add acai puree and baby spinach. Add raw cacao nib powder, strawberries, sliced banana and almond milk and pulse till smooth. Transfer the smoothie into a large serving glass. Top with raw cacao nib and serve immediately.

Acai & Berries Smoothie

Makes: 1 serving

Ingredients:

- ½ cup blueberries
- 1 cup strawberries
- 1 tablespoons cacao powder
- 1 cup acai juice
- 1 cup almond milk

For Topping:

- 2 large fresh mint leaves
- 3 to 4 berries

Procedure:

In a high speed blender, add blueberries and strawberries. Add cacao powder, acai juice and almond milk and pulse till smooth. Transfer the smoothie into a large serving glass. Top with mint leaves and berries and serve immediately.

Acai & Spinach Smoothie

<u>Makes:</u> 1 serving

Ingredients:

- ½ cup frozen acai berry puree
- 1 cup strawberries
- 1 tablespoon cacao nib powder
- ½ cup coconut milk
- 1 cup torn fresh spinach
- ½ of peeled and sliced small banana
- ¼ cup crushed ice cubes

<u>For Garnishing:</u>

- 2 small fresh spinach leaves

Procedure:

In a high speed blender, add acai berry puree, strawberries and cacao nib powder. Add coconut milk, spinach, sliced banana and ice cubes and pulse till smooth. Transfer the smoothie into a large serving glass. Garnish with spinach leaf and serve immediately.

Acai Berry & Pomegranate Smoothie

Makes: 1 serving

- ½ cup frozen acai berry puree
- ½ cup coconut milk
- ½ cup pomegranate seeds
- 1 peeled, cored and chopped large green apple
- 1 of peeled and sliced small banana
- ¼ cup crushed ice cubes

For Topping:

- 2 tablespoons pomegranate seeds

In a high speed blender, add acai berry puree and coconut milk. Add pomegranate, apple, sliced banana and ice cubes and pulse till smooth. Transfer the smoothie into a large serving glass. Top with pomegranate and serve immediately.

Acai Berry & Cherry Smoothie

Makes: 1 serving

Ingredients:

- ½ cup frozen acai berry puree
- 1 cup fresh cherries
- 1 of peeled and sliced small banana
- 1 tablespoon cacao nib powder
- 1 cup almond milk
- ¼ cup crushed ice cubes

For Topping:

- 1 or 2 fresh cherries
- 1 tablespoon shredded coconut
- 1 tablespoon cacao nibs

Procedure:

In a high speed blender, add Acai berry puree, and cherries. Add sliced banana, cacao nib powder, almond milk and ice cubes and pulse till smooth. Transfer the smoothie into a large glass. Top with cherries, shredded coconut and cacao nibs and serve immediately.

Acai & Peanut Butter Smoothie

Makes: 1 serving

Ingredients:

- ½ cup frozen acai berry puree
- 1 tablespoon peanut butter
- 1 of peeled and sliced small banana
- ½ cup almond milk
- ¼ cup crushed ice cubes

For Topping:

- ½ of peeled and sliced small banana

Procedure:

In a high speed blender, add acai berry puree and peanut butter. Add sliced banana, almond milk and ice cubes and pulse till smooth. Transfer the smoothie into a large serving glass. Top with banana slice and serve immediately.

Acai Berry & Coconut Smoothie

Makes: 1 serving

Ingredients:

- ½ cup frozen acai berry puree
- 1 teaspoon agave]
- ½ cup coconut water
- ½ cup coconut milk
- ¼ cup crushed ice cubes

For topping:

- 1 tablespoon shredded coconut

Procedure:

In a high speed blender, add acai berry puree, agave, coconut water, coconut milk and ice cubes and pulse till smooth. Transfer the smoothie into a large serving glass. Top with shredded coconut and serve immediately.

Acai Berry & Kale Smoothie

Makes: 1 serving

Ingredients:

- ½ cup frozen acai berry puree
- 1 cup kale leaves
- 1 peeled, cored and chopped apple
- 1 peeled and sliced small banana
- ¼ cup blueberries
- 1 cup coconut milk
- ¼ cup crushed ice cubes

For Topping:

- 2 large fresh mint leaves

Procedure:

In a high speed blender, add acai berry puree and kale leaves. Add chopped apple, sliced banana, blueberries, coconut milk and ice cubes and pulse till smooth. Transfer the smoothie into a large serving glass. Top with mint leaf and serve immediately.

Acai Berry & Strawberry Smoothie

Makes: 1 serving

Ingredients:

- ½ cup frozen acai berry puree
- ½ cup strawberries
- 2 of peeled and sliced small bananas
- ½ cup almond milk
- ¼ cup crushed ice cubes

For Topping:

- ¼ cup strawberries
- ¼ cup blackberries
- 2 large fresh mint leaves

Procedure:

In a high speed blender, add acai berry puree and strawberries. Add sliced banana, almond milk and ice cubes and pulse till smooth. Transfer the smoothie into a large serving glass. Top with strawberries, blackberries and mint leaves and serve immediately.

Acai Berry & Pineapple Smoothie

Makes: 1 serving

- ½ cup frozen acai berry puree
- ¼ cup pineapple juice
- 1 of peeled and sliced small banana
- ½ cup almond milk
- ¼ cup crushed ice cubes

For Topping:

- 1 slice of pineapple

Procedure:

In a high speed blender, add, acai berry puree and pineapple juice. Add sliced banana, almond milk and ice cubes and pulse till smooth. Transfer the smoothie into a large serving glass. Top with pineapple slice and serve immediately.

Acai Berry & Chia Seeds Smoothie

<u>Makes:</u> 1 serving

Ingredients:

- ½ cup frozen acai berry puree
- 1 tablespoon Chia seeds
- 1 of peeled and sliced small banana
- ½ cup almond milk
- 1 tablespoon goji berry juice
- ¼ cup crushed ice cubes

<u>For Topping:</u>

- 2 tablespoons goji berries
- 1 tablespoon chia seeds

Procedure:

In a high speed blender, add, acai berry puree and Chia seeds. Add sliced banana, almond milk, goji berry juice and ice cubes and pulse till smooth. Transfer the smoothie into a large serving glass. Top with goji berries and chia seeds and serve immediately.

Acai Berry & Carrot Smoothie

Makes: 1 serving

Ingredients:

- ½ cup frozen acai berry puree
- ¼ cup carrot puree
- ¼ cup mango puree
- ¼ cup strawberries
- 1 of peeled and sliced small banana
- ½ cup almond milk
- ¼ cup crushed ice cubes

For Topping:

- ¼ cup berries (black and red)

Procedure:

In a high speed blender add acai berry puree, carrot puree and mango puree. Add strawberries, sliced banana, almond milk and ice cubes and pulse till smooth. Transfer the smoothie into a large serving glass. Top with berries and serve immediately.

Two Awesome Free Gifts For You

I want to say "Thank You" for buying my book so I've put together a few, awesome free gifts for you.

The Essential Kitchen Series Cooking Hacks & Tips Book

&

100 Delicious New Recipes

These gifts are the perfect add-on to this book and I know you'll love them.

So visit the link below to grab them now!

www.GoodLivingPublishing.com/essential-kitchen

49344833R00025

Made in the USA
San Bernardino, CA
21 May 2017